BY RUTH ROGG

Orlando　Boston　Dallas　Chicago　San Diego

Visit *The Learning Site!*
www.harcourtschool.com

The eggs most people eat are laid by hens. Farmers sell the eggs as food. Most hens don't hatch their own eggs.

Most birds sit on their eggs until they are ready to hatch. Most eggs have the same shape. The sizes and the colors of eggs can be very different.

The ostrich lays the largest bird egg. A nest is shared by a few ostrich mothers. They all lay their eggs in the same nest. The mothers take turns sitting on the eggs in the daytime. The father sits on the nest at night.

An emperor penguin mother lays one round egg and goes into the sea to eat.

The father penguin takes care of the egg through the miserable, cold Antarctic winter. He rolls the egg onto his feet. Then he stays close to other fathers on the slippery ice to keep the egg warm.

The father feeds the chick until the mother comes back. Then he goes off to the sea to find food.

The father penguin waddled away to eat. Now it's the mother's turn to care for the chick.

The mother sea horse puts her eggs into the father's pouch. Like the penguin father, the sea horse father cares for the eggs until they hatch.

This fish carries the eggs in its mouth until they hatch.

Most fish lay their eggs in the water. Some eggs float and others sink. Fish eggs are called roe.

Some fish protect their eggs. Others do not.

Most shark eggs hatch inside the mother. A few kinds of sharks, like the bullhead shark, lay eggs in the sea. These eggs fall to the sea floor and stay between rocks until they hatch.

This shark's eggs have strong cases and twisted edges.

Most frogs lay their eggs in the water. These eggs do not have a shell. They are covered with a kind of jelly that helps protect them.

Some frogs lay more than one thousand eggs at a time. Most of the eggs get eaten by fish. The rest of the eggs can hatch into tadpoles.

Young frogs are called tadpoles.

A mother sea turtle crawls out of the sea to lay her eggs. The turtle digs a hole on the beach. She lays her eggs in the hole. Then she covers the eggs with sand and goes back to the sea. Heat from the sun warms the eggs.

A mother turtle crawls out of the ocean to lay her eggs in the sand.

The young turtles are on their own. The sun on the horizon helps guide them back to the sea. They swim off by beating their flippers like birds flapping their wings.

This snake has a sharp egg tooth that helps it break out of its egg.

Most snakes lay eggs. They dig holes in the sand or make nests for the eggs. Most snake mothers leave their eggs to hatch on their own.

A mother grasshopper digs a hole in the ground. She lays eggs in the hole and covers them with soil. The eggs are called a pod.

When young grasshoppers hatch, they look like their parents but have no wings.

caterpillar egg

A mother butterfly carefully chooses the type of plant to put her eggs on. A tiny caterpillar comes out of the egg. It begins to eat the leaves of the plant. It grows and changes before it looks like a butterfly.